Getting Started

Even in this day of microwave ovens and fast foods, the kitchen remains an important part of all our lives. It also provides a place where hands-on math occurs anytime you cook.

Brainstorm

Ask "Did you know that cooks have to use math?" "Why do you think we need to know math in order to cook?" List every idea your students name. Guide them through questioning to create a complete list.

- measuring ingredients
- deciding how much you need
- determining if you have enough
- telling time/temperature as you cook
- purchasing ingredients
- adjusting recipes

Ask

"Who cooks in your house?"
"Do you ever cook?"
"What do you cook?"
"Where do people cook besides at home?"

Explain that you are going to be doing some cooking and other activities to show how important math is in something we are a part of everyday.

©1994 by Evan-Moor Corp.

What is in Your Kitchen?

Search
Reproduce the "In Our Kitchen" form on page 3. Have children take the form home to use as they take a close look at their own kitchens to find examples of the use of math. When the forms are returned, spend some time discussing the results.

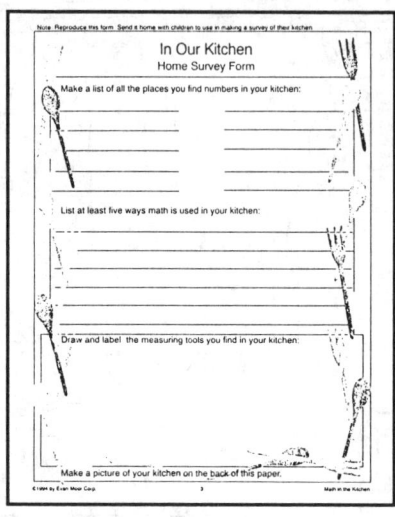

Interview
Reproduce the interview sheet on page 4 for children to use as they interview their favorite cook. Model the activity by having children ask you (or provide a cook to stand in) the questions on the form. When the interview sheets are returned, spend some time sharing the information students have gathered.

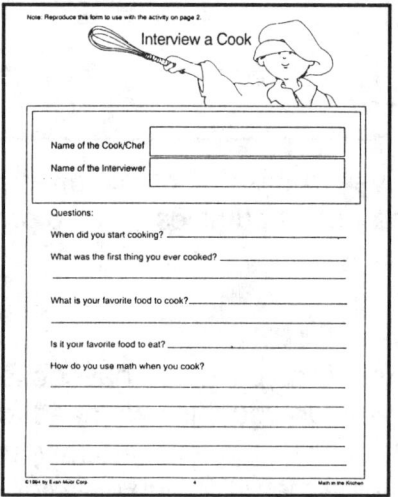

Speakers
Invite cooks from different areas to speak to the class about how they learned to cook, how they use math when they cook, what happens if you make a mistake in your math when cooking, etc.

- a class parent
- a cafeteria cook
- a cook from a local restaurant
- someone from a bakery

Make Portfolios
Have children prepare working portfolios to use as they complete activities in this unit. Give each child a file folder containing a pocket or have them make a portfolio from a sheet of construction paper. Have them decorate the cover in a "cooking" motif and add their names and the date the unit begins. Provide a safe (but accessible) place for the portfolios when the children are not using them.

Note: Reproduce this form. Send it home with children to use in making a survey of their kitchen.

In Our Kitchen
Home Survey Form

Make a list of all the places you find numbers in your kitchen:

_____   _____
_____   _____
_____   _____
_____   _____
_____   _____

List at least five ways math is used in your kitchen:

_____
_____
_____
_____
_____

Draw and label the measuring tools you find in your kitchen:

Make a picture of your kitchen on the back of this paper.

©1994 by Evan-Moor Corp.   Math in the Kitchen

Note: Reproduce this form to use with the activity on page 2.

Interview a Cook

Name of the Cook/Chef	
Name of the Interviewer	

Questions:

When did you start cooking? _____

What was the first thing you ever cooked? _____
_____

What is your favorite food to cook? _____
_____

Is it your favorite food to eat? _____

How do you use math when you cook?

_____
_____
_____
_____

©1994 by Evan-Moor Corp.

Using Kitchen Tools

Do the following activities with your class to help them understand how kitchen tools are used and which tool is best for a task.

Name and Explain
Place a selection of implements on a table. Ask children to identify the implements. Invite a child to come up and explain what the tool is used for and/or demonstrate what it does.

Which is Best?
Explain that the utensil used for the same task can change over time. New inventions and methods are developed. Use the following demonstration to show how progress usually saves time, but often costs more.

   1. Beating egg whites can be done in several ways. Select three children to come up and demonstrate. Give one a fork, one a whisk, and one an electric egg beater (under close supervision or do this yourself). Give each a bowl containing the white of an egg. Demonstrate how they are to use their utensils to beat the egg white. Say "Start when I say go. Go!"

   2. When the first egg white forms peaks say "Stop." Have children compare the results. Provide time for another try if you have children who feel they could do it just as fast with the fork or whisk as with an egg beater.

   3. Ask "Which worked the fastest?" "Which do you think costs the most money?" "Is it more important to be fast or inexpensive?"

Cooking Utensils

Set up an area for your students to examine and explore a variety of small kitchen utensils. Bring in the real tools if you possibly can. If you bring in sharp items or those requiring heat or electricity, demonstrate their use, then put them in a safe place to be taken home. Many kitchen items can be left out for children to handle.

Once children can name the utensils and know what they are used for, add some computation task cards to the area. The difficulty of the skills covered should reflect the needs of your class.

Spatula – $1.50
Wooden spoon – $1.00
Whisk – $4.00
Tongs – $2.50

Put up a chart showing prices for the various pieces of equipment. Place a set of word problem cards in the center for children to read and solve.

Put out a household catalog and/or some kitchen ads. Have children list two items (or more) that they would like to have in their kitchen, look up the cost of the items, and add to find the total.

Reproduce page 7 for each child. Have children name the items and explain their use.

Note: Reproduce this page to use with the third activity on page 6.

Kitchen Tools

What is it? How is it used?

©1994 by Evan-Moor Corp.   7   Math in the Kitchen

Classroom Cooks

Encourage classroom discussion.

> What did you have for breakfast today? Who cooked it for you? Did you make your own lunch? Do you cook at home? What kinds of things? How do you help? Who taught you? Do you like to cook?

> What do you need to know in order to cook?

> I need to know:
> how to read directions
> how to measure
> safety rules

> How do you clean up after you cook? What kinds of things do you need to do? Why is it important to keep the kitchen and food clean?

> Do you know how much food costs? Do your parents ever tell you something in the store costs too much? Is the most expensive thing the best tasting?

Explain that the class will be learning about the cost of foods and will be cooking in several different ways:
- together as a class
- in small groups
- individually or in pairs in centers

Note: Send this form home to be completed by the student as he/she cooks something at home.

Home Cooking Experience

Who cooked: _____

_____

We cooked _____ together.

We used this equipment:

This is how we made it:

We used math these ways:

A Center
Let's Shop

This center provides the opportunity for children to become comparison shoppers and to practice various math skills as well as use their reading and comprehension abilities.

Collect empty cereal boxes, soup cans, and various cookie packages. Put price tags on each container. Provide pencils and paper for children to use to record their answers.

Make a set of question cards to go in the center. You can change the questions each week in the center to make it a different challenge each time a child works at it. Write the questions on file cards or cards cut from tag. Here are some sample questions. The skill level needs to be adapted to the level of your students. You can use pictures, words, or a combination of both. Actual names of products and prices will depend on the items in your center.

How much does one bag of cookies cost?

How much would three bags cost?

How much does one box of cereal cost?

How much would ten boxes cost?

Pretend you have one dollar. List what you can buy.

Choose one can of soup, one package of cookies, and one box of cereal.
a. What is their total cost?
b. If you paid for them with a 20 dollar bill, how much change would you get back?

Pick two bags of cookies. Write down the cost of each can or bag. What is the difference in the price?

You need cookies for a dozen children. Look at the cost of the cookies and at how many servings are in the box. Which package is the best buy?

©1994 by Evan-Moor Corp.   Math in the Kitchen

Note: Reproduce this page for children to do at home with their parents.
Use the results as part of your discussion of comparison shopping.

My Favorite Breakfast

I ate:

cost:

total cost

Who fixed your breakfast? _____

Cost Comparisons

Explain that a grocery store or supermarket has many brands of the same type of food. Talk about national brands, store brands, and generic items. These may cost many different prices. Do one or more of the following cost comparison activities.

1. Bring in three versions of the same kind of cereal. Pour out a sample of each in a dish. Mark the dish with the cost of the cereal. Compare the prices. Repeat this process with several other items.

2. Bring in a few weeks' worth of grocery ads from the newspaper. Put students into groups of four for this activity. Give each group a few sets of ads and have them look through to see if they can find the same general item for different costs. Use the form on page 13 to record the prices.

Discuss the findings as a class. Ask children to think about whether the items are different in any way.

3. Take a field trip to a supermarket to make price comparisons. Have each group of students look at the prices of one item. You will need to have a parent along with each group to help with supervision and to assist with reading labels and prices and for help in recording data. Ask older or more able students to look for a name brand, store brand, and generic brand for the item they are observing.

Note: Use the version most appropriate to the task your students are doing. Model the process before students work independently.

Cost Comparison

We looked for _____

Brand 1 _____ cost _____

Brand 2 _____ cost _____

Brand 3 _____ cost _____

- -

Cost Comparison

We looked for _____

Brand name _____ cost _____

Store brand _____ cost _____

Cost difference [ ]

©1994 by Evan-Moor Corp.   13   Math in the Kitchen

Taste Tests

Discussion
Explain "When I watch television or read magazines I see ads telling me that one soft drink tastes best, or one kind of peanut butter is best." Ask "Do you think one brand tastes better than any other?" "What is the best brand of _____?" Allow time for your students to offer their reasons. List the brands they say are best. Have each child come up and put a tally mark by the one they think is best. See if there is an overall favorite.

A Blind Taste Test
Design a taste test for a few items to compare the tastes of well-known national brands, store brands, and generic items (peanut butter, sodas, ice cream, etc.).

Use the same flavor for each item you are testing (all colas, all vanilla ice cream, etc.) so colors are the same. Label the three samples 1, 2, 3 or A, B, C. Fill the containers behind a screen so children cannot get clues from containers.

Have children record their choices on the form on page 15.

Tally the amount of students that prefer each brand. Discuss the results. Ask "Did the one most people liked cost the most?" "If something costs more does it taste better?"

Extension
Figure out how much you save by buying lesser-known brands.

Taste Test Ballot

Date _____

Name _____

1. Taste
2. Think
3. Choose

What was being tasted: _____

Brands tasted:

Notes:

Which brand would you choose?

[_____]

Why?

_____

_____

_____

_____

Advertising Campaign

Discussion
Ask children to describe their favorite television ads. See how many can sing the commercial song or repeat the slogan. Ask "Why are ads on television and in magazines?" See if they can come up with the idea that advertisements are to try and get you to buy something. Ask "Is everything you hear or see in an advertisement true?" "Have you ever seen or heard an ad and bought the thing?" "Was it as good as the ad said?"

Think About Ads
Explain that the words and pictures used are chosen to try to get us to buy that product. Video tape some ads or bring in magazine ads. Guide children through an analysis of what the ad is trying to do and of its words and claims. Are the ads true...exaggerated...a lie?

Create an Ad
Choose a kind of food. Divide children into groups of four. Ask them to design an advertisement for the food. One part of the campaign needs to be in print, and the other needs to be live, as in a television commercial. Give each group a chance to present their campaign to the rest of the class.

Measurement

Before children are ready to cook, they need to understand how to measure liquid and dry ingredients. Have them work in groups of four to practice measuring ingredients using water or rice. Cover work areas with pieces of heavy duty plastic or oilcloth. Have paper towels handy for spills. Give each group a set of measuring cups and measuring spoons (the same activities can be done using standard US measurement or metric measurement - both types are represented on the forms on pages 18 and 19). Include a plastic knife for leveling off dry ingredients. You will be giving some directions orally for the groups to follow.

How many _____ in a cup?
Make comparisons using either water or rice.

Each group will need a copy of the measuring worksheet on page 18 and a set of measuring cups. Give the directions orally. Assign the students in each groups the numbers 1, 2, 3, and 4 as a way to rotate students through the work. Have students work around a small desk so they can pass the utensils easily and so they can all see what is happening. Here's a sample of the way to manage the session.

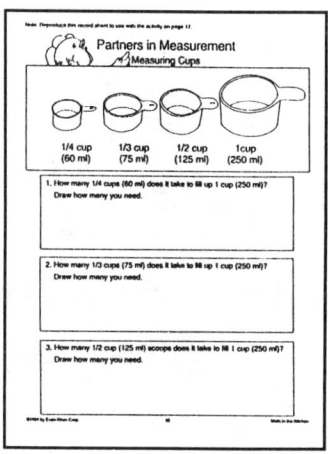

Teacher:
"Person Number 1, fill the 1/4 cup (60 ml) and pour it into the 1 cup (250 ml). Draw a picture of the 1/4 cup (60 ml) on the worksheet. Is the 1 cup (250 ml) full?" (No)

Continue the same directions and questions for person number 2 and 3 in the group.

"Number 4, fill up the 1/4 cup (60 ml) and pour it into the 1 cup (250 ml). Draw another 1/4 cup (60 ml) on your group's worksheet. Did that fill the 1 cup (250 ml)?" (Yes) "How many 1/4 cups (60 ml) are in 1 cup (250 ml) ?" (four)

Have each group continue the activity using the 1/3 measuring cup (75 ml) and the 1/2 measuring cup (125 ml) following the same procedure as above.

How many _____ in a teaspoon?
Give each group a copy of the worksheet on page 19. Have them follow the same procedure to make comparisons using measuring spoons.

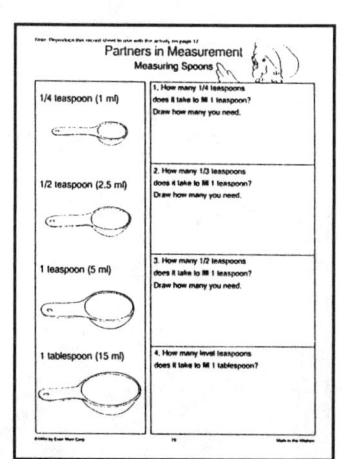

©1994 by Evan-Moor Corp. Math in the Kitchen

Note: Reproduce this record sheet to use with the activity on page 17.

Partners in Measurement
Measuring Cups

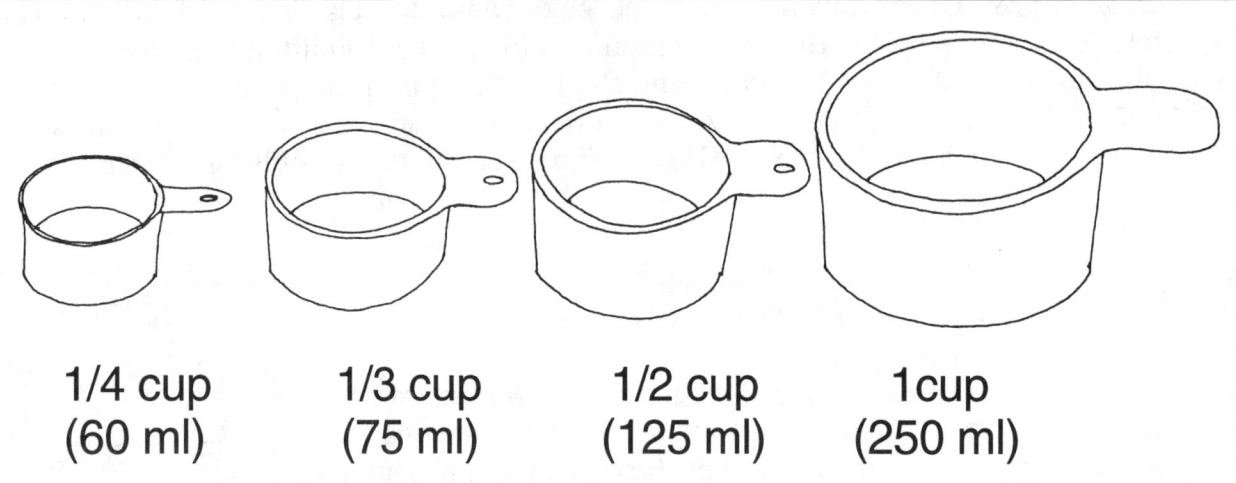

1/4 cup (60 ml)   1/3 cup (75 ml)   1/2 cup (125 ml)   1 cup (250 ml)

1. How many 1/4 cups (60 ml) does it take to fill up 1 cup (250 ml)? Draw how many you need.

2. How many 1/3 cups (75 ml) does it take to fill up 1 cup (250 ml)? Draw how many you need.

3. How many 1/2 cup (125 ml) scoops does it take to fill 1 cup (250 ml)? Draw how many you need.

©1994 by Evan-Moor Corp.   Math in the Kitchen

Note: Reproduce this record sheet to use with the activity on page 17.

Partners in Measurement
Measuring Spoons

1/4 teaspoon (1 ml)

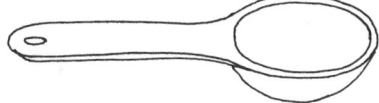

1. How many 1/4 teaspoons does it take to fill 1 teaspoon? Draw how many you need.

1/2 teaspoon (2.5 ml)

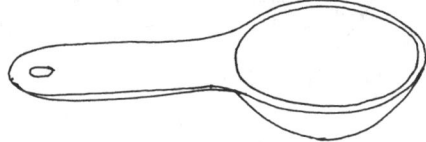

2. How many 1/3 teaspoons does it take to fill 1 teaspoon? Draw how many you need.

1 teaspoon (5 ml)

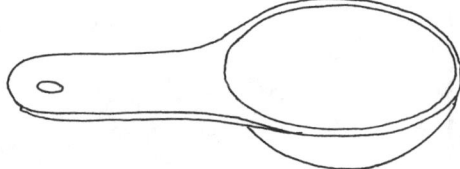

3. How many 1/2 teaspoons does it take to fill 1 teaspoon? Draw how many you need.

1 tablespoon (15 ml)

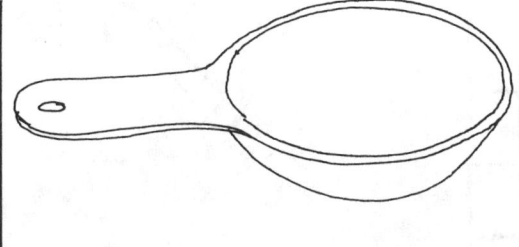

4. How many level teaspoons does it take to fill 1 tablespoon?

©1994 by Evan-Moor Corp.   Math in the Kitchen

Graph What You Know

Have children work in pairs. Give them sheets of 1" (2.5 cm) graph paper to create graphs showing the relationships between fractions of cups and cups. Complete a second graph to show the relationships between the various sizes of measuring spoons. Model the process on the chalkboard before having children begin their own graphs.

Fraction Graph for Measuring Cups

| 1 | 1/2 | 1/3 | 1/4 |

Fraction Graph for Measuring Spoons

| 1/4 tsp | 1/2 tsp | 1 tsp | 1 tbsp |

Simple Cooking Experiences

Centers

Check with parents to find out if any of your children have food allergies you need to consider in planning cooking and eating activities.

None of the cooking centers require a heat source; however, some do require milk and other items which need to be keep cool. You will need a good cooler or access to a refrigerator for these items. Put out the recipe ingredients just before the time children will be using these centers.

Before you begin the cooking centers, decide how you will rotate children through the centers and when you will have center cooking time. Set up behavior standards and clean-up procedures. Post these in the area where you have placed the centers.

Materials may be kept in a central location with children collecting what they need or they may be kept at the individual centers. You may want to provide aprons and cooks' "hats" for your chefs to wear while cooking.

Recipe cards are included for four cooking centers. You can change or add to these to make them more appropriate for your particular students.

Use one of the suggested center cooking experiences to model procedures before children begin working independently. Have children follow these steps.

1. Read the recipe card.
2. Gather supplies.
3. Cook.
4. Eat.
5. Clean up the area.

Show students tips such as using a plastic knife to make level spoon or cup measurements. Go through each center and read the recipe, discussing the process they will follow, and answering questions.

The cooking activities on the center cards are very simple. If you have access to a portable oven and/or microwave oven, and you feel your students are ready, create your own cards containing more elaborate experiences (making muffins, simple soups, etc.).

Extensions

Have students practice adding sums of money as they work through the cooking centers. Post a copy of page 24 with the centers. Write the cost of each item in its box. These costs will depend on the brands you purchase for the centers. Reproduce the forms on page 25 and cut them apart. Children select the form for the center they will be using, fill in the cost for the items, and add to find the total cost.

©1994 by Evan-Moor Corp.   21   Math in the Kitchen

Note: These "recipes" are meant as individual experiences.

Instant Pudding

You need:
- measuring spoon
- measuring cup
- jar with lid
- plastic spoon
- paper cup
- plastic knife
- 4 level tablespoons (60 ml) pudding mix
- 1/2 cup (125 ml) milk

Steps:
1. Put the pudding mix and milk in the jar.
2. Put the lid on the jar. Shake the jar as you count to 50.
3. Pour the pudding into the paper cup. Let it sit for one minute.
4. Eat your pudding.
5. Clean up your work area.

Peanut Butter and Jelly Sandwich

You need:
- plastic knife
- measuring spoon
- 1 slice of bread
- 2 level tablespoons (30 ml) peanut butter
- 2 teaspoons (10 ml) jelly

Steps:
1. Spread peanut butter on the bread.
2. Spread jelly on the bread.
3. Cut the bread in half like this. What shape did you make?
4. Eat your sandwich.
5. Clean up your work area.

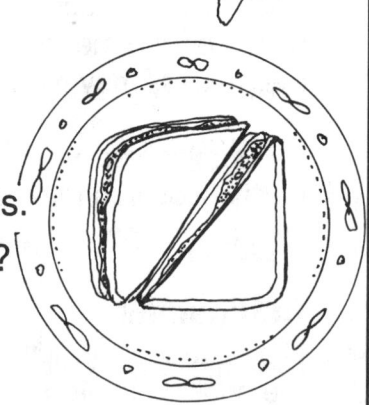

Fruit Drink

You need:
- glass
- spoon
- measuring cup
- measuring spoon
- plastic knife
- 4 level Tablespoons (60 ml) drink powder
- 2/3 cup (150 ml) water

Steps:

1. Pour water into your glass.

2. Add the drink powder. Stir until it is all mixed in.

3. Enjoy your drink.

4. Clean up your work area.

Snack Mix

You need:
- measuring spoon
- measuring cup
- paper cup
- 1 Tablespoon (15 ml) raisins
- 1/4 cup (60 ml) cereal
- 1 dozen pretzel sticks

Steps:

1. Put your raisins and cereal in the paper cup. Mix them up.

2. Add the pretzel sticks.

3. Eat your snack.

4. Clean up your work area.

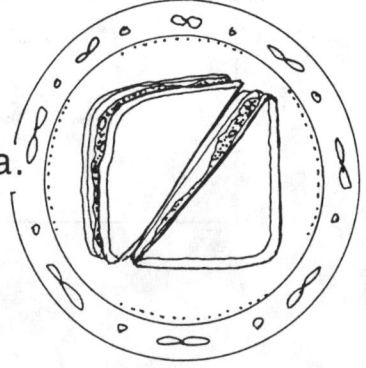

What Would it Cost?

Post a list of items and costs by the cooking center area. Have children calculate the cost of what they need to prepare the "recipe" before beginning the actual cooking activity.

pudding mix - ☐ cents per tablespoon (15 ml)

milk - ☐ cents per cup (250 ml)

bread - ☐ cents per slice

peanut butter - ☐ cents per tablespoon (15 ml)

jelly - ☐ cents per teaspoon (5 ml)

drink powder - ☐ cents per tablespoon (15 ml)

water - ☐ cents per 1/3 cup (75 ml)

raisins - ☐ cents per tablespoon (15 ml)

cereal - ☐ cents per 1/4 cup (60 ml)

pretzel sticks - ☐ cents per stick

©1994 by Evan-Moor Corp.   Math in the Kitchen

Cost of Pudding

4 tablespoons
(60 ml) pudding mix

1/2 cup (125 ml)
milk

Cost of Sandwich

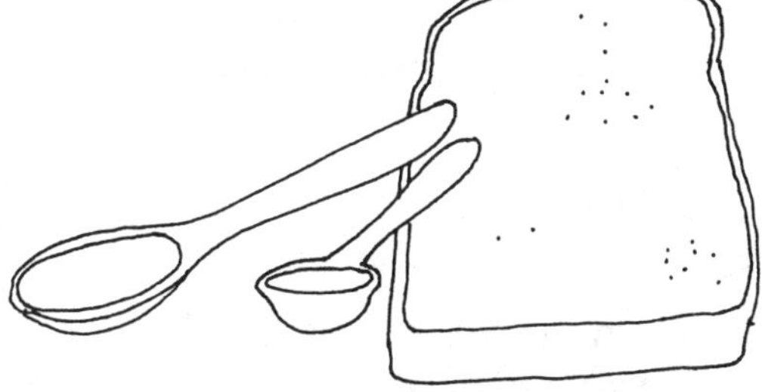

1 slice bread

2 tablespoons
(30 ml) peanut butter

2 teaspoons jelly
(10 ml)

Cost of Fruit Drink

4 tablespoons
(60 ml) drink mix

2/3 cup (150 ml)
water

Cost of Snack Mix

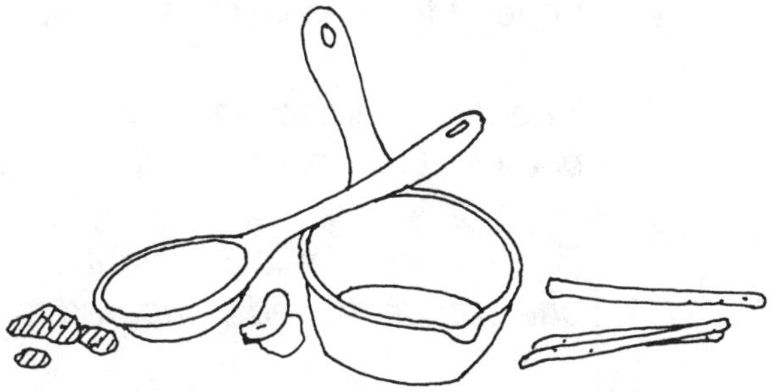

1 tablespoon (15 ml)
raisins

1/4 cup (60 ml) cereal

1 dozen pretzels

Note: This cooking activity is for the whole class.

Popcorn

Popcorn makes a great math-in-cooking activity. Do this as a whole group experience calling on children to help you do each step. Children may work independently or in pairs to answer some of the questions as you go along.

You will need popcorn, a popcorn popper, a kitchen scale, and plastic drinking cups as you go through the following activities.

Activities

- Figure out how many cups of popped corn you will need for everyone in class to have two cups.

- Estimate how many cups of unpopped kernels will make that amount. Have each child write his/her estimate on a kernel-shaped piece of paper and appoint someone to keep a tally of how many cups you use. Refer back to this estimate after you have popped the necessary amount of popcorn.

- Find the difference in volume.
  one half cup unpopped is ___ cups popped

- Find the difference in weight.
  one cup unpopped compared to one cup popped

- Figure out -
  How many kernels were unpopped in one cup of popcorn? How many kernels popped in one cup of popcorn?

- Find how many unpopped kernels of popcorn fit along a one-foot (30.5 cm) line? How many unpopped kernels will fit on the same line?

Extension
Read Tomie de Paola's ***The Popcorn Book*** as children enjoy their popcorn snack.

Cookies

Brainstorm with your class to create a list of all the types of cookies your children can name. Write these on the chalkboard or chart paper. Have each child come up and put a tally mark beside his/her three favorite kinds. Graph the results of this survey.

Have children look at the list again and ask "Which of these cookies has anyone you know made at home?" Circle these. Explain that they will be baking "school-made" cookies. Either use the chocolate chip cookie recipe included in this book, your own favorite recipe, or have your students look at the circled cookies and vote on which type they would like to bake.

The following cooking activity is based on chocolate chip cookies. If your class wants to make a different kind, replace the recipe on page 29 with the appropriate one for your group and make a new set of task cards (see page 34).

Cookie Ingredients
Cost Comparisons

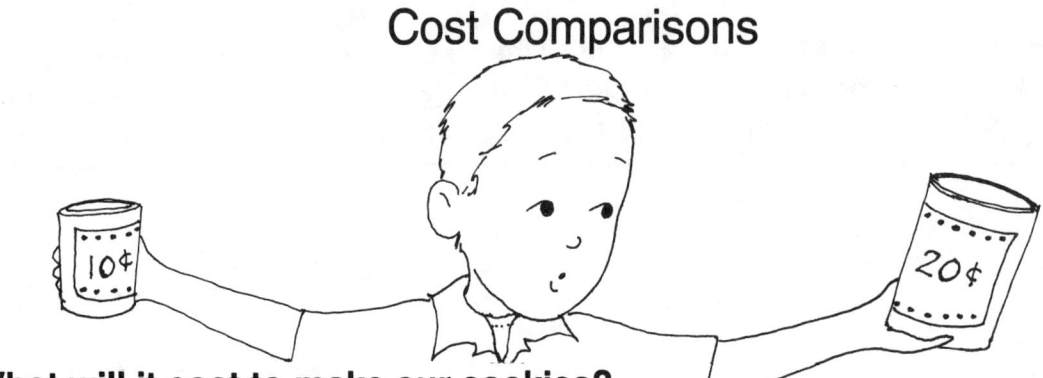

What will it cost to make our cookies?
Give each group a copy of the cookie recipe on page 29 and the cost comparison sheet on page 30.

A field trip to the grocery store is in order, but if that's not possible, you can have three different brands of the items in the recipe sent in by volunteers (with the prices clearly listed, since in today's computer-scanning age, the price is not always visible on the package).

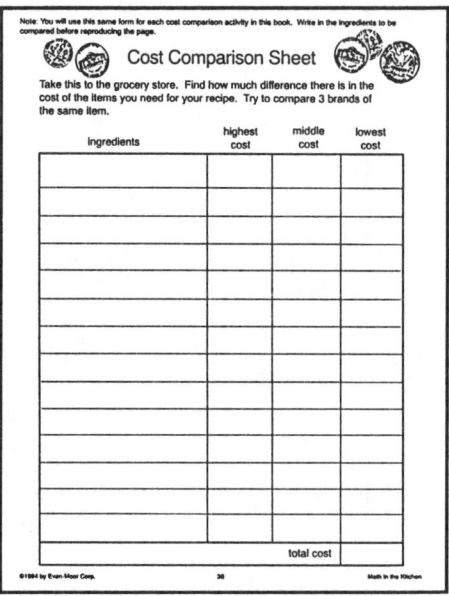

If you can go to the store, try to have an adult along for each group to assist with supervision and to help children reading prices, quantities, etc. Discuss how the store is set up and look at the aisle markers to help find the items. There are nine items on the recipe list. This can be too much for one store visit so you may want to limit the comparisons to the main ingredients (chocolate chips, sugar, butter, flour). Have students compare three different brands of each item, making sure the quantities are the same. The three prices are to be written on the worksheet in the appropriate column.

When you return to the classroom, have the groups add up the columns. Use this system if your students are adding large numbers in a column.

- have one child add up the numbers manually
- have the next child check the answer manually
- have the next child add up the same column of numbers with a calculator
- the last child also checks with a calculator

If children are not ready to do these large numbers manually, have them each add the numbers on a calculator and see if they all get the same total.

Use the information they gathered to decide which brands will be the most economical to buy.

©1994 by Evan-Moor Corp.   Math in the Kitchen

Note: This baking activity is done in groups of four.

Chocolate Chip Cookie Recipe

Ingredients:
- 1/2 cup (125 ml) butter
- 1/2 cup (125 ml) brown sugar
- 1/2 cup (125 ml) white sugar
- 1 tsp. (5 ml) vanilla extract
- 1 egg
- 1/4 tsp. (1 ml) salt
- 1/2 tsp. (2.5 ml) baking soda
- 1 1/8 cup (275 ml) flour
- 1 cup (250 ml) chocolate chips

Steps:
1. Preheat oven to 375 degrees fahrenheit (190 Celsius).
2. Soften the butter.
3. Add brown and white sugars and stir well.
4. Add egg and vanilla to the sugar and butter.
5. Mix together flour, salt, and baking soda.
6. Add flour mixture to butter-sugar-egg mixture.
7. Mix well.
8. Stir in chocolate chips.
9. Put on cookie sheet in one tablespoon drops.
10. Bake for 10-12 minutes.
11. Cool for 2 minutes, then take off cookie sheet to finish cooling.

Note: You will use this same form for each cost comparison activity in this book. Reproduce a blank copy. Write in the ingredients to be compared. Then reproduce the page for students.

Cost Comparison Sheet

Take this to the grocery store. Find how much difference there is in the cost of the items you need for your recipe. Try to compare three brands of the same item.

ingredients	highest cost	middle cost	lowest cost
		total cost	

©1994 by Evan-Moor Corp.   Math in the Kitchen

Planning for Cooking

This activity is to encourage thoughtful planning and problem solving. Divide children into groups of four. Give each group a copy of the recipe you are planning to make, a blank sheet of paper and copies of the parent letter on page 32.

Each group has two jobs:
1. They must list on the blank paper all of the utensils they think their group will need to make the recipe.
2. Then they must assign those utensils to members of their group. Each person will fill out a letter to his/her parents asking them to loan the utensils the group needs.

The class as a whole may then share their compiled lists to see if there are any discrepancies in what the groups perceive as needed utensils.

Note: Reproduce this form to use with the activity on page 31.

_____
date

Dear _____,

Our group is going to bake cookies in class. Can you help by sending the following utensils for us to use? We will take good care of everything and they will be returned when we are finished with the lesson.

_____

_____

_____

Thank you for your help.

        Sincerely,

        _____

  # Cooking Cookies

Gathering Supplies
Review the list of utensils made in the preceding lesson. Be sure each group has everything they need.

Give each group a task list from page 34. Review the steps and explain how children are to take turns doing the different parts. Each child signs his/her name to the step when it has been completed. Discuss how they will measure out 1/8 cup of flour in step 9.

Mixing Cookies
Review the recipe. Have each group collect the ingredients they need from a central area. Have them mix the ingredients following the steps on the task cards.

How Many Cookies?
After the cookies have been mixed, but before putting them on the cooking sheet, pass out cookie shapes cut from construction paper and have children do this lesson in estimation.

Using a tablespoon (15 ml spoon), have one child in each group scoop out one cookie and place it on the baking sheet. Have each child write down his/her estimate of how many cookies the recipe will actually make on the paper cookie.

Discuss what might happen if the cookies are scooped either too large or too small. Have the group take turns scooping out cookie dough and placing it on the cookie sheet. When they are done, have them count the number of cookies they actually made and compare it to their estimate. Also compare to see if all the groups have about the same number of cookies. If not, discuss the possible reasons for not having the same number.

Baking Cookies
Mark each baking pan with washable marking pen, so each group gets the correct pan back. Bake the cookies in a portable oven or in the school cafeteria (if your cooks are agreeable). Cool. Return the cookies to their groups. Have children divide the cookies evenly among the group. This may mean cutting some cookies into fractional parts to come out evenly. Provide baggies for children to use to carry their cookies home. Have them label their bags to avoid confusion.

Extension
Have children come back into their same groups to complete their cooking journals. Give each group a copy of the form on page 35, plus the group's set of task cards. Have them write down what they did. Have each child write his/her section of the cooking experiment.

Note: Give each group a copy of these tasks to follow as they make their cookies.

Cookie Task List

Sign here.

1. Measure the butter. Put it in a bowl. Stir it until it is creamy.	
2. Measure 1/2 cup (125 ml) of brown sugar. Press it into the cup. Stir it into the butter.	
3. Measure 1/2 cup (125 ml) of white sugar. Stir it into the butter.	
4. Measure 1 teaspoon (5 ml) of vanilla extract. Put it the bowl. Stir it in.	
5. Crack one egg into the bowl. Don't get any shell in the bowl. Stir to mix.	
6. Measure 1/2 teaspoon (2.5 ml) of baking soda into a different bowl.	
7. Measure 1/4 teaspoon (1 ml) of salt. Put it in with the baking soda. Stir.	
8. Measure 1 cup (250 ml) of flour. Put it in with the soda and salt. Stir.	
9. Measure 1/8 cup (30 ml) of flour. Put it in with the flour, salt and soda. Stir.	
10. Pour the flour mixture into the butter mixutre. Stir until the flour is all mixed in.	
11. Measure 1 cup (250 ml) of chocolate chips into the bowl. Stir in.	
12. Check the recipe to make sure it's all in the bowl.	

©1994 by Evan-Moor Corp. Math in the Kitchen

Note: Reproduce this form to use with any cooking experience in this book.

_____ Cooking Journal
name

Name of Recipe:

The steps my group followed:

_____
_____
_____
_____
_____
_____
_____
_____

How I used math in this recipe:

_____
_____
_____

Note: Use this activity for practicing math skills, then contribute the full cookie jar to a good cause (the teachers' lunchroom, cafeteria cooks as a thank-you, a house bound person in the neighborhood, a nursing home, etc.).

How Many Cookies in the Cookie Jar?

After your students' cookies have baked and cooled, collect a portion of the cookies to go in a cookie jar (which can be a large glass jar or decorated coffee can). Do the following activities with the cookies:

1. Select someone to keep a tally of the cookies as they are collected. Write the total number on the chalkboard.

2. Place one cookie in the jar. Using that information, ask students to estimate how many cookies the jar will hold. Provide tongs or plastic gloves for handling the cookies. Select a student to put the cookies in the jar. Have children count as the cookies are put inside. Compare estimates to the total number the jar holds.
- Have children calculate the difference between their estimate and the number in the jar.
- If one cookie jar has _____ cookies, how many cookies would be in two jars? five jars? ten jars?

3. Use the total number of cookies collected (see number one) to do the following type of problems. Select those appropriate to the needs of your students. Allow students to use paper and pencil, drawing, real objects, etc., to solve the problems.
- How many dozen cookies were there?
- If we divide the cookies into two equal parts, how many will be in each half? If we divide the cookies into fourths?
- If each person in the room ate one of the cookies, how many would be left?
- How many cookies would we need if every boy in our class ate two cookies? if every girl ate five cookies?
- If it cost ten cents to make one cookie, how much would 10 cookies cost? two dozen cookies? a cookie for each person in our room?

Dozen, Dozen, How Many Dozen?

Brainstorm to create a list of things we might buy by the dozen (cookies, eggs, rolls, fruit, etc). Use these items as the starting point for practicing counting, computation, and fractions. The activities below use cookies and eggs, but you could use any item that comes in dozens.

How many dozen do we need?
Have your students work in pairs. Ask "How many dozen cookies do we need for everyone in our class to get one cookie?" (two cookies, three cookies, etc.?) Provide time for each pair to share how they figured out the problem (drew pictures, divided, made people and cookie shapes, etc.).

How many dozen in 100?
Divide children into small groups. Ask "How many dozen are in 100?" Provide counters, construction paper and scissors, whatever they might use to figure out this problem. When they are finished, see how many different ways they used to find the answer.

A Dozen Eggs
Bring in empty egg cartons and plastic eggs (or other small objects). Set these out with a set of problem cards appropriate to your grade level. Use the cartons and eggs as manipulatives to solve the problems.
- How many eggs are in two dozen? three dozen? etc.
- Use the egg cartons to help you count by twelves to 144.
- How much is 1/2 a dozen? 1/3 a dozen? 1/4 a dozen? etc.
- How many dozen will 36 eggs make? 24? 60? etc.

Note: The basic steps for making pizza are the same as baking cookies. You will be using some of the same forms.

Let's Make Pizza

Read *Pizza for Breakfast* by Maryann Kovalski (Morrow Junior Books; 1991) to your students as an introduction to activities involving pizza.

Making pizza is a more complicated process than baking cookies. Several variations are given for creating the crust. Select the one that fits your class and time allotments best.

Before putting children into groups, brainstorm to make a list of the items they like on their pizza. Put this list on the board. Working together, figure out the combinations of ingredients (no more than three on a pizza) that can be made from the ingredients on the class list. (If their list is too long, take a "favorite kind" tally to limit the number of items you have to work with.) Start with no topping (counting plain cheese pizza as "no topping"), then list all the toppings you have, then combine two toppings, etc. This teaches systematic listing skills.

no toppings	1 topping	2 toppings
cheese	pepperoni	pepperoni and mushroom
	mushroom	pepperoni and olives
	olives	pepperoni and sausage
	sausage	mushroom and olives
		mushroom and sausage
		olives and sausage

What Kind of Pizza Will We Make?
To decide what type of pizza to make, have children cut out three small pizza shapes from construction paper (see below). Have them put their name on each pizza.

Put one of the pizza combinations on a separate index card, and spread them out. Have each child vote for the three types of pizza they would like. Narrow this down until you have groups of four wanting to make the same type of pizza.

Preparing the Dough

The first decision you need to make is whether you want to attempt making pizza crust from scratch with your students. It can be done, but it is an involved process.

You may prefer to use a packaged mix which will still require measuring activities but can be accomplished faster. The simplest of all is to use prepared pizza crust and anchor your math experiences around the toppings you use and dividing the pizza for eating.

Once you have determined what type of pizza crust to make and what toppings will be needed, divide students into groups to make cost comparisons (form on page 30) and to list cooking equipment they will need (form on page 32).

Dough from "Scratch"

Early in the morning, have the children make the pizza dough, using the recipe on page 40. Pass out the task cards (page 41) as you did in the cookie activity. Each child will get to knead the dough for one minute. Bring in an egg timer and use this opportunity to think about the length of one minute.

Roll the dough into the pizza pans and cover to let the dough rise.

While the dough is rising, have children draw a picture to show the top of the pizza and the pattern they will make with their toppings.

When the dough has risen, the sauce, cheese and toppings can be added and the pizza taken to the ovens to bake.

When the pizzas are done, let them cool.

Note: This baking activity is done in groups of four.

Pizza Recipe

Ingredients:
- 1 cup (250 ml) warm water
- 1 package active dry yeast
- 2 to 3 cups (500 - 750 ml) flour
- 1 1/2 tablespoons (17.5 ml) vegetable oil
- 1/2 teaspoon (2.5 ml) salt
- pizza sauce
- shredded Mozzarella cheese
- assorted toppings

Steps:
1. Put yeast in warm water. Stir well. Wait 5 minutes. It should be foamy.
2. Add 2 cups (500 ml) of flour. Stir with wooden spoon.
3. Add salt with hands. Then add 1 tablespoon (15 ml) of oil.
4. Knead the dough, adding a little more flour as you go, until it is not sticky anymore. Add more flour if it is still sticky.
5. Cover the bowl and let the dough rise in a warm place for 2 hours. After 2 hours, flatten the dough out onto the pizza pan.
6. Put oil around the edges of the pizza crust. Cover again and let sit for 30 minutes.
7. Add pizza sauce, cheese and toppings.
8. Bake at 375 degrees Fahrenheit (190 degrees Celsius) for 30 minutes. Let it cool.

Note: Individualize this task list to match the recipe you are using.

Task List for Pizza

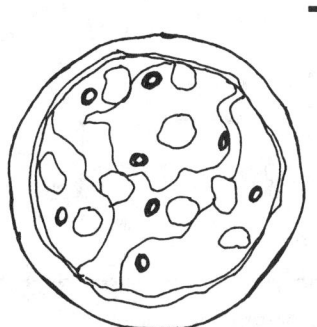 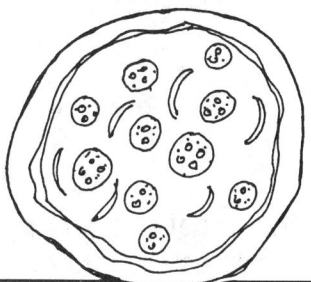 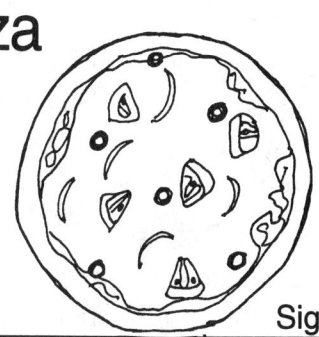

Task	Sign here.
1. Measure 1 cup (250 ml) of warm water into the bowl.	
2. Put the package of yeast into the bowl. Stir. Wait 5 minutes.	
3. Measure 2 cups (500 ml) of flour into the bowl. Stir with spoon.	
4. Measure 1/2 teaspoon (2.5 ml) of salt into the bowl. Mix in.	
5. Measure 1 tablespoon (15 ml) of oil into the bowl. Mix in.	
6. Put 1/4 cup (60 ml) of flour on the table. Knead for one minute.	
7. Put 1/4 cup (60 ml) of flour on the table. Knead for one minute.	
8. Put 1/4 cup (60 ml) of flour on the table. Knead for one minute.	
9. Put 1/4 cup (60 ml) of flour on the table. Knead for one minute.	
10. Check to make sure the dough isn't sticky. Cover the bowl.	
11. After 2 hours, put the dough into the pizza pan.	
12. Put oil around the edges of the crust. Cover for 30 minutes.	
13. Put the sauce on the pizza.	
14. Put the cheese on the pizza.	
15. Put the toppings on the pizza.	
16. Tell your teacher the pizza is ready for the oven.	

©1994 by Evan-Moor Corp.

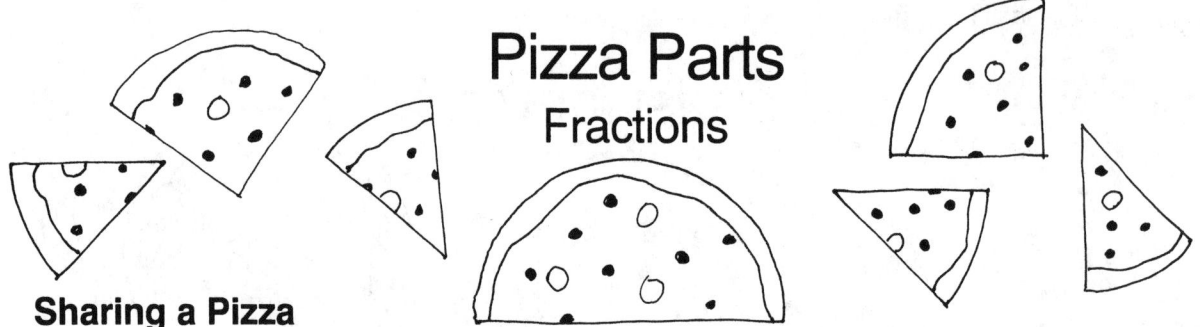

Pizza Parts
Fractions

Sharing a Pizza
Give each student a sheet of drawing paper and a copy of the recording form on page 43. Have them draw their favorite pizza as big and round as possible, then cut the pizza out. Follow these steps to divide it into fractional parts.

1. Have children look at the top half of the record sheet. Ask "Can you tell me what we could call the first circle on our page?" Explain that it is a whole thing, just like the pizza circle is a whole pizza. Have them color in the whole and write 1 under it.

2. Have children fold the circle in half, open it up, and draw a line with crayon or marking pen along the fold line. Ask "What do we call one side of the pizza?" (one half) "Look at the next pizza on your record sheet. Color in one half of the circle and write 1/2 under it."

3. Have children refold the pizza into halves, then fold it again to make fourths. Repeat the directions in step 2 for fourths and for eighths.

When the children's own pizzas are cool enough to eat, help them divide their own pizzas into eight parts, two for each person in the group.

Solving Pizza Word Problems
Use the bottom half of page 43 to practice word problems with fractional parts. Make the problems as easy or complicated as is appropriate for your students. Give the problems orally. Have children record their answers by coloring in the answer on the pizza. Remind children that everyone has two pieces of pizza. They need to remember this as they figure out the answers.

1. _____ finished his pizza. Color in how much he ate. Write the fraction next to the pizza.

2. _____ and _____ ate all of their pizza. How much did they eat together?

3. _____ ate his pizza and half of _____'s. How much did he/she eat?

4. _____ went home before we ate the pizza. The rest of his group ate all of their pizza. How much did they eat?

5. _____ ate all of her pizza. _____ ate one piece of her's. _____ ate all of his. How much pizza was left?

6. _____ and _____ each ate 1/4 of a pizza. How much pizza was left?

©1994 by Evan-Moor Corp.   Math in the Kitchen

Note: Reproduce this page to use with the activities on page 42.

Pieces of Pizza

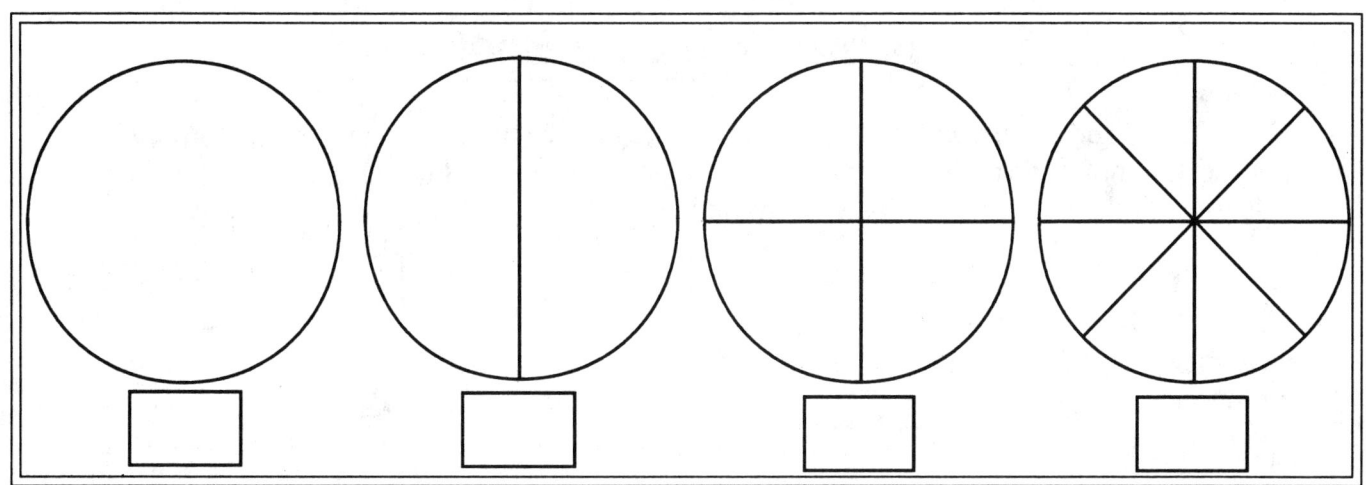

Word Problems

1. /8
2. /8
3. 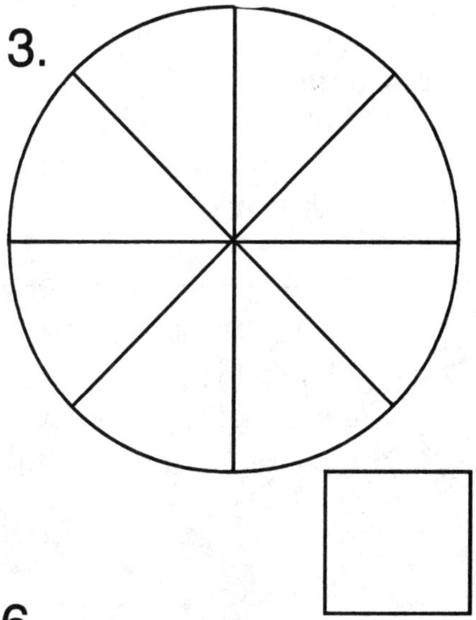
4. 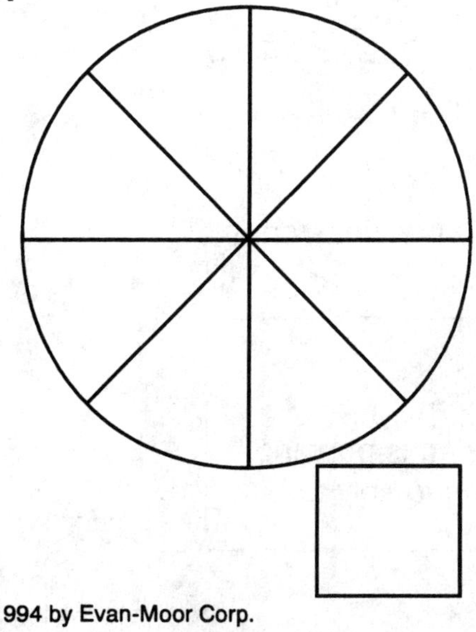
5. 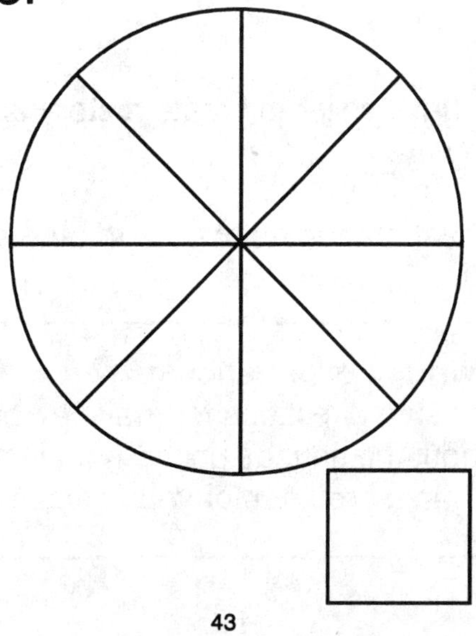
6.

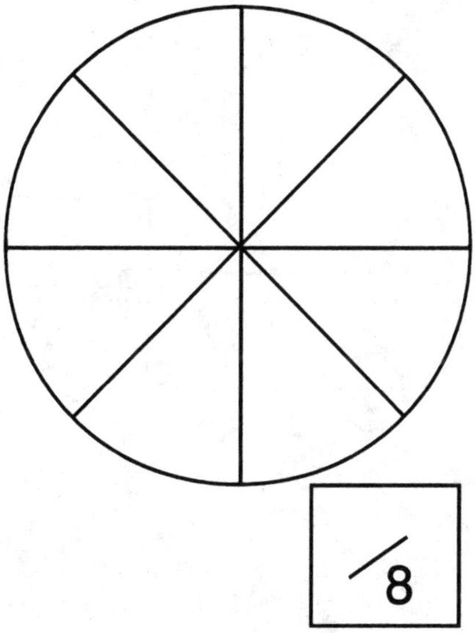

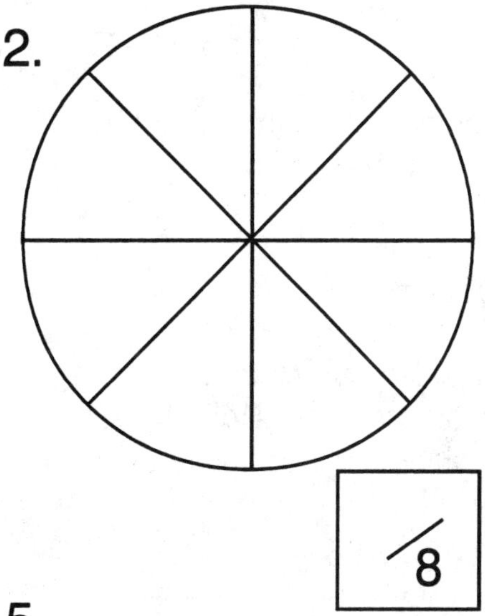

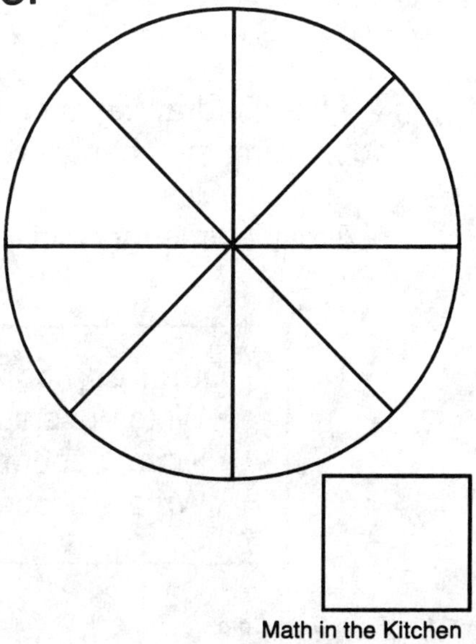

Language Extensions

Make "Food" Books

Popcorn *Unfolding* Book

Read **The Popcorn Book** by Tomie de Paola. Compare the scientific explanation and the old American Indian legend that tells why popcorn pops. Have students write about this topic and share their stories with friends.

Materials:
- 9" X 12" (23 X 30 cm) white construction paper
- crayons
- writing paper

Steps:

1. Fold the construction paper in half. With the fold at the bottom, fold down the top piece as shown in the illustration.

2. Draw the popped kernal of corn.

3. Unfold the paper. On the inside have children draw what they think makes the corn pop. Refold the paper and pull it open to show the surprise.

4. After the drawing is done, have children create a story about why popcorn pops using the character they drew.

5. Provide time for children to share their stories with others in the classroom.

Other pop corn writing experiences:
- Write out step-by-step directions for making popcorn.
- Write a poem about the sounds popcorn makes as it is popping.
- Write a popcorn math problem for your classmates to solve.

Three-Fold Cookie Book

Read **My Grandmother's Cookie Jar** by Montzalee Miller to your class. Discuss how we save memories of special people and times. Guide them through the steps to make a *three-fold* cookie book.

Materials:
- 6" X 18" (15 X 45.5 cm) brown construction paper
- 3" X 5" (7.5 X 13 cm) writing paper
- crayons, pencil
- scissors
- paste
- stapler

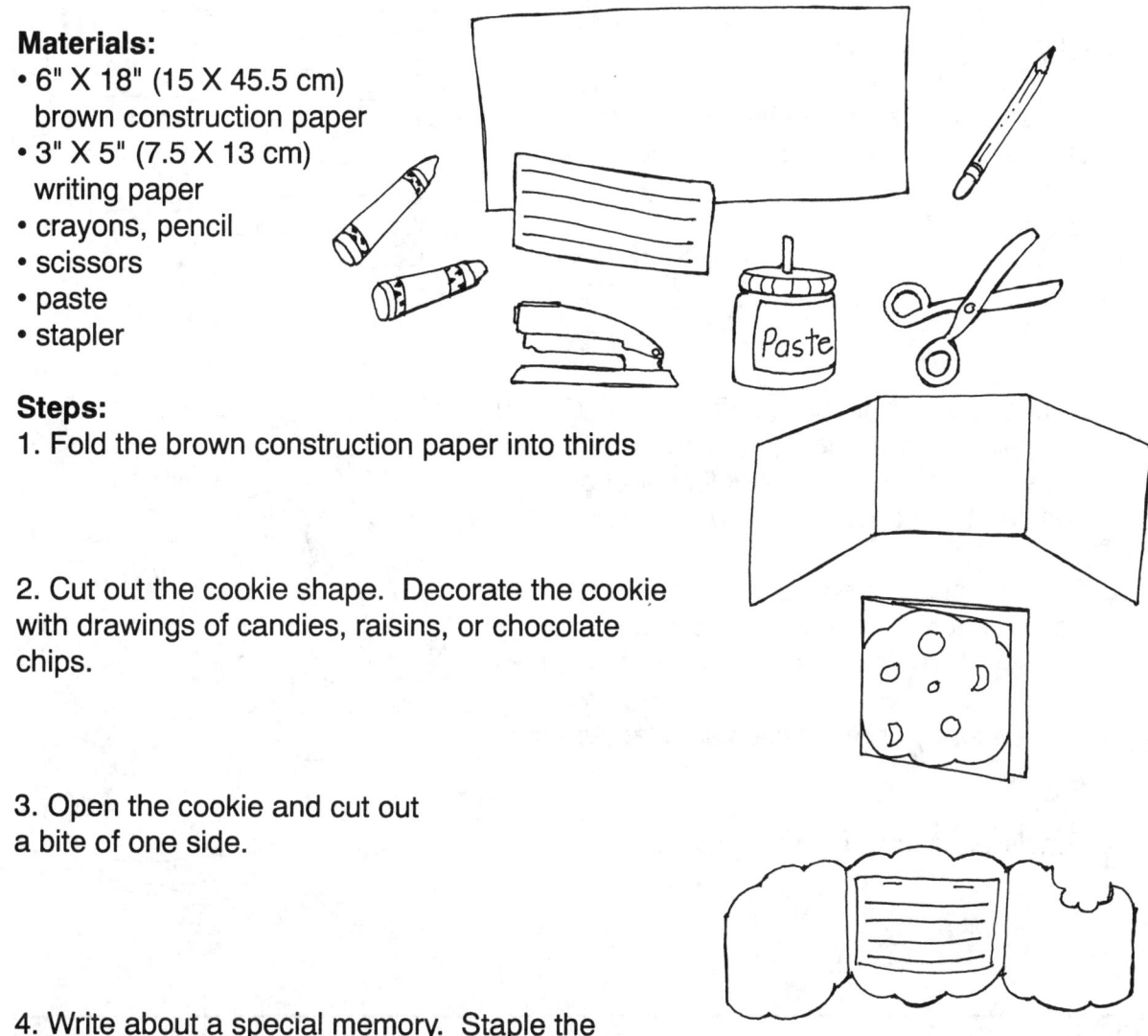

Steps:
1. Fold the brown construction paper into thirds

2. Cut out the cookie shape. Decorate the cookie with drawings of candies, raisins, or chocolate chips.

3. Open the cookie and cut out a bite of one side.

4. Write about a special memory. Staple the "memory" paper inside the cookie.

Display the cookies on a bulletin board for everyone to read.

Other cookie writing experiences:
- Write a description of the smell and taste of a cookie fresh from the oven.
- Write your favorite cookie recipe. (These can be collected into a class cookie recipe book.)
- Write a riddle about your favorite cookie. Put the riddle on the first page. Put the answer on the inside.
- Write a cookie math problem for your classmates to solve.

©1994 by Evan-Moor Corp.

Pizza Shape Book

Read *Pizza for Breakfast* by Maryann Kovalski to your class. Ask them how they feel about the idea of having pizza for breakfast. What might be on that pizza?

Materials:
- white construction paper
- writing paper (as many sheets as needed by students)
- crayons or marking pens
- pencil
- stapler
- scissors

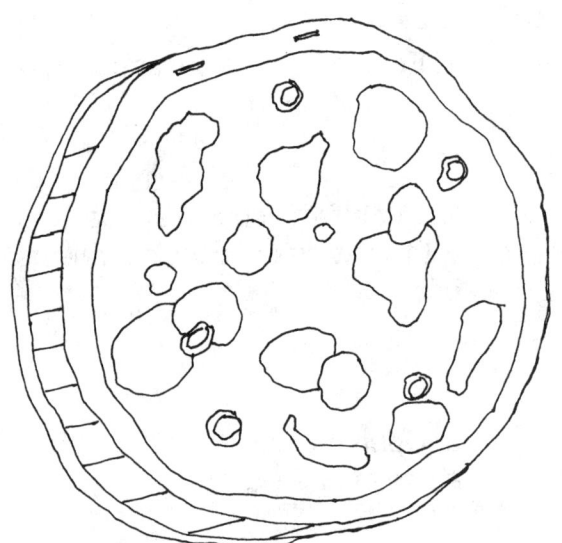

Steps:
1. Take one sheet of construction paper. Cut out a rough circle by rounding corners. Use this as a pattern for cutting out the other sheet of construction paper and the writing paper.

2. Color in one sheet of construction paper or paste on torn construction paper pieces to look like your favorite pizza. This is the front cover.

3. Write a funny or mysterious story about your pizza.

4. Staple the story inside the pizza cover.

Other pizza writing ideas:
- Write a description of your pizza. Use as many descriptive words as you can.
  - How does it look?
  - How does it smell?
  - How does it sound?
  - How does it taste?
- Write a recipe for your favorite pizza.
- Make an alphabet of pizza words. Put one word on each page. Make a picture to illustrate the word. Can you think of something for every letter?

  a - anchovy......................*a smelly anchovy*
  b - bacon............................*sizzling bacon*
  c - cheddar cheese............*gooey cheese*

Art Extension
Pasta People

Pasta comes in wonderful shapes and sizes. Use this activity to combine art and math. Children will be required to measure the pasta they will be using and to calculate what the cost of the materials would be.

Place materials in an accessible area. Post a chart containing the "costs" of materials. Provide paper and pencils for calculating and recording material costs. The chart should reflect the skill level of your students.

Materials:
- pasta of various kinds
- glue
- construction paper in various colors
- measuring cups and spoons
- pencils
- recording sheet (page 48)

Directions:
1. Discuss the types of "people" students might make (princess, football player, giant, alien from space, etc.).

2. Explain the process they are to follow.
   a. Sketch the person with pencil on the construction paper.
   b. Collect materials by measuring out the various types of pasta he/she needs to fill in the sketch keeping track of how many spoons or cups they take. Refer to the "cost chart" and figure out how much the materials cost.
   c. Count each type of pasta in a spoon or cup. Record this number.
   d. Lay our the pasta to fill in the person sketch. Arrange the pieces to be sure you like the look, then glue the pieces down.
   e. While the glue dries, count the pasta of each type that is left. Record these numbers on your form. Figure out the difference.

Extension: Have children name their pasta person, then write a story about him/her/it.

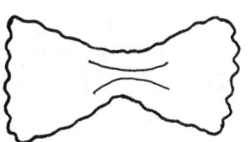
Bow ties

Macaroni

Thimbles

Rotini

Wagon wheels

Shells

Stars

Linguini

Pasta People
Recording Sheet

Type of Pasta	Cost for each	Number of pasta pieces I took	Number of pasta pieces I used	Difference

Pasta People
Recording Sheet

Type of Pasta	Cost for each	Number of pasta pieces I took	Number of pasta pieces I used	Difference

©1994 by Evan-Moor Corp.   Math in the Kitchen